BR PARCELS and PASSENGER-RATED STOCK

Volume 2

Horse Boxes, Special Cattle Vans and Vehicles for Fish, Fruit and Milk Traffic

David Larkin

BR PARCELS AND PASSENGER-RATED STOCK – VOLUME 2

©Kestrel Railway Books and David Larkin 2015

Kestrel Railway Books
PO Box 269
SOUTHAMPTON
SO30 4XR

www.kestrelrailwaybooks.co.uk

All rights reserved.

No part of this publication may be
reproduced, stored in a retrieval system,
transmitted in any form or by any means,
electronic, mechanical, or photocopied,
recorded or otherwise, without the
consent of the publisher in writing.

Printed by the Amadeus Press

ISBN 978-1-905505-34-0

Front cover (top left): M42520M, possibly taken at Carlisle Citadel on an unknown date, with crimson livery. (Photograph courtesy HMRS, Ref ABW230)
Front cover (top right): M38999, taken at Birmingham Snow Hill, post-1969, with crimson livery. (Courtesy HMRS, ref ABW213)
Front cover (bottom left): MMB42846, taken at Swindon on 13th March 1989, with silver/ blue livery. (Authors Ref No W15748/DL)
Front cover (bottom right): M40312, taken at Millerhill Yard in the 1960s, with freight bauxite livery. (Photograph by Don Rowland, courtesy S4 Society)

Back cover (top left): E87045, taken at Sheffield in August 1968, with ice blue livery. (Author's Ref No W1038/DL)
Back cover (top right): S3732S, taken at an unknown location and date, with SR green livery. (Photograph by David Welch, Author's Ref No W1888/DL)
Back cover (bottom left): W92030W, taken at an unknown location and date, with crimson livery. (Courtesy HMRS, Ref AEL721)
Back cover (bottom right): S3287, taken at Andover Junction on 18th August 1952, in weathered crimson livery. (Photograph by AE West, courtesy Mike King (Wessex Collection))

HORSE BOXES, SPECIAL CATTLE VANS AND VEHICLES FOR FISH, FRUIT AND MILK TRAFFIC

Contents

Introduction iv

Code Letters, Numbering and Livery 1

BR Period Overview 3

Wagon Descriptions
    HB (Horse Boxes) 8
        Former LMS designs 9
        LNER origins 11
        SR origins 16
        GWR origins 17
        BR Standard Mk 1 Horse Boxes 18
    Fish Vans (All designs) 20
        LMS designs 21
        GWR designs 24
        LNER and BR designs 26
        Passenger Diagram Vans 31
    Fruit Vans (Passenger Rated) 44
    Special Cattle Vans and Calf Boxes 49
        SR-designed stock 52
        GWR-designed stock 54
    Palethorpes Royal Cambridge Sausage Vans 56
    Milk Traffic 58
        Milk products 59
        Milk churn traffic 60
        Mobile Tank Carriage Trucks (for towed road milk tanks) 66
        Milk Tanks (fixed-tank designs) 68
        Express Dairy Co Ltd 69
        United Dairies Co Ltd / United Dairies (Wholesale) Co Ltd / Unigate Creameries Ltd / St Ivel 73
        Co-operative Wholesale Society Co Ltd / London Co-operative Society 80
        Cow & Gate Ltd 82
        Independent Milk Supplies Ltd 82
        Nestle-Anglo Swiss Ltd 82
        Milk Marketing Board 84
        Milk Marketing Board (post-1981 fleet) 86
    Conclusion 88

BR PARCELS AND PASSENGER-RATED STOCK – VOLUME 2

Introduction

I last approached the subject of parcels and associated rolling stock in 1978 and, due to the fact that I had concentrated on freight rolling stock, I had to use illustrations from others sources and those showing vehicles being used for "engineering" duties.

In the intervening period, not a lot has changed although I do now have enough material to produce a two-volume work.

All parcels trains required a vehicle in which the guard travelled, and there was usually space for a parcels-related load as well. This volume will look at the various livestock vehicles, such as the horse boxes and special cattle vans, and perishable-traffic vehicles for fish, fruit and milk. It will also look at how the above traffics were carried, whether by parcels train, or by block trains of one commodity, or whether by passenger train as an attached vehicle at either the front or the rear.

Acknowledgements are due to the Historical Model Railway Society for extensive use of photographs from their collection. Thanks are also due to Mike King for photographs from the Wessex Collection of AE West and to John Talbot who took many views in the Worcester area. As ever, my thanks to Jean for her work in typing lists back in the 1970s and 1980s without which I could not produce these books.

David Larkin, December 2014

HORSE BOXES, SPECIAL CATTLE VANS AND VEHICLES FOR FISH, FRUIT AND MILK TRAFFIC

Code Letters, Numbering and Livery

Parcels-rated stock was given a short code that was painted on the side of the vehicle concerned. Codes relevant to Volume 2 are as follows:

BM: Milk Van, sometimes with guard's compartment
HB: Horse Box
SCV: Special Cattle Van
FRUIT D: Four-wheeled Fruit Van of GWR design
SIPHON: Milk van of ex-GWR design, with identifying code letter
BLOATER: Fish Van of GWR origin with 18ft 0in wheelbase
FISH: Fish Van with 12ft 0in wheelbase or under
INSIXFISH: Six-wheeled Insulated Fish Van
INSULFISH: Four-wheeled Insulated Fish Van
XFISH: Six-wheeled Fish Van

Unlike freight vehicles, passenger vehicles used the prefix letter (that is, **E**=Eastern/ North Eastern, **M**=London Midland, **S**=Southern, **Sc**=Scottish and **W**=Western) to denote regional allocation. The suffix letter (that is, **E**=LNER design, **M**=LMS design, **S**=SR design and **W**=GWR design) indicated design origin. If there was no suffix, this usually indicated a B standard design, although this could not always be relied upon.

All vehicles in 1948 kept their original liveries until BR decided on crimson with yellow lettering for all parcels stock; this is also referred to as carmine red by many sources. Some BG vans, however, were used as extra luggage vans in long-distance passenger trains received crimson and cream (that is, "blood and custard") livery. When standard BR BG, CCT and GUV vans were introduced, later examples were line maroon.

From 1956, the Southern Region was allowed to paint its vehicles green and this was applied to parcels vans as they passed through carriage works.

Fish vans were something of a special case and some designs were actually freight vehicles. They were, however, suitable for passenger train working and have been included in the volume. Early liveries wavered between freight bauxite and passenger crimson before settling on the former.

Insulated fish vans were a different matter and they initially received the freight livery of white livery with black lettering. Some received the post-1966 ice blue livery with black lettering. When no longer being used for fish traffic, some later received rail blue livery and even freight brown livery

From the late 1960s, the handful of survivors in the HB or SCV had weathered crimson or, in the case of the Southern Region stock, green livery.

The GWR designs, the FRUIT Ds and SIPHON Gs, carried rail blue livery in later years.

Finally, the milk tanks were a special case. Only the chassis was owned by BR and this was always black. Tank colour depended on the operator and will be fully explored in the text. These vehicles did not carry a code, except for the late flowering of the design with the Milk Marketing Board. This somewhat surprising event will also be explored fully in the relevant text.

As with the vehicles covered in Volume 1, the suffix letters began to disappear in the mid-1970s, as TOPS had by then become universal, rendering them unnecessary.

W44560, taken at St Erth in April 1970, is in the simple St Ivel orange livery and is operated by Unigate Creameries, one of the two main operators in BR days. (Author's Ref No W2514/DL)

BR Period Overview

The traffics carried by the vehicles studied in this volume were much more specialized and each traffic had a different fleet.

Taking things in alphabetic order, we must look at the Horse Box fleet. This is extremely complicated and will be examined in more detail in the main text. Suffice to say at this time that BR inherited a comparatively modern fleet from the LMS, a very motley fleet of pre-Grouping vehicles and modern types, which remained in production as late as 1955, from the LMS and LNER, a few pre-Grouping vehicles from the SR and a mixed fleet from the GWR, many of which carried calves rather than horses in BR days.

To this fleet was added BR's own Mk 1 Horse Box design, which in fact saw very little use.

S96369, taken at the National Railway Museum, York in June 1978, was a BR Mk 1 standard horse box allocated to the Southern Region, despite the fact that clearance issues restricted its use. It is seen here is SR green awaiting restoration. (Author's Ref No W6944/DL)

Fish traffic was handled by the LMS, LNER and GWR, the SR not having the ports for trawlers and drifters. Both of the two northern companies blurred the issue as to which stock was freight only or passenger-rated but, in essence, such traffic in the BR period was passenger-rated and all vehicles will be studied here.

The LMS had both four-wheeled designs and six-wheeled designs, both of which saw use in the early 1950s, including some six-wheeled vans built in 1949. With the arrival of more-modern LNE-inspired stock, the four-wheeled stock passed quickly into freight services as ordinary vans, few surviving beyond 1965 as passenger rated vehicles. The six-wheeled vans were barred from passenger trains from 1959 and were steadily withdrawn thereafter.

The LNER fleet leant heavily on freight designed four-wheeled vans in the 1930s and even went to extent of converting many of these to insulated fish vans.

E229210, taken at Millerhill Yard in the 1960s, is a Diagram 134 fish van converted to insulated fish van and carrying white livery with black lettering. Note the prominent steam-heating pipe for working on passenger trains. (Photograph by Don Rowland, courtesy S4 Society)

HORSE BOXES, SPECIAL CATTLE VANS AND VEHICLES FOR FISH, FRUIT AND MILK TRAFFIC

The next vehicles to appear totally revolutionized fish traffic in BR days. The first design was also a freight diagram, Diagram 214, and six hundred were built.

This batch was followed by a further five hundred vehicles in 1954. This group had the same bodywork but were retrospectively fitted with roller bearings. They were also numbered in the passenger series. Finally a further five hundred and fifty seven vans were built to a slightly modified design from 1957 onwards fitted with roller bearings from new. This fleet, collectively, took over fish traffic until it was lost in the 1970s.

The GWR had a curiously obsolescent fleet of four-wheeled vans which saw some BR use until swept away by the vehicles noted above. The only modern vans were a small batch of fifty vehicles built in 1948. These were six-wheeled insulated vehicles which ended up being transferred to the Scottish Region.

DE75305, taken at York in August 1968, is a Diagram 214 which has now been downgraded to a stores van, although retaining white livery. This batch was also fitted with steam pipes for passenger train working, and also kept oil axleboxes. The end vents were added after the van was downgraded. (Author's Ref No W422/DL)

Fruit traffic was carried in freight vehicles on the LNER system and, to a lesser extent, by the LMS The SR used elderly pre-Grouping parcels vans then standard PMVs and CCTs for the relatively short journeys they needed to service.

The GWR, which had lots of fruit traffic, especially from the Vale of Evesham in Worcestershire, developed a fleet of four-wheeled vans with slatted sides and ends for extra ventilation. The vans became longer, with extra doors, and metal vents replaced the end slats, but essentially the design remained the same. All were passenger-rated.

W92073, taken at Wisbech in September 1969, has received rail blue livery and is clearly marked PASSENGER. It is also marked MAXIMUM SPEED 45 MPH, an instruction issued after a serious derailment. (Author's Ref No W1804/DL)

One batch was built in the early days of Nationalisation but this was probably a GWR order being fulfilled.

More surprising was the authorisation of two further batches, one apparently built in 1956 and one, of which W92073 above was a part, as late as 1960, by BR In truth, these vehicles were the Western Region equivalent of the Southern Region PMV and used on normal parcels for most of the year. Subsequently, Western Region took deliveries of standard Mk 1 CCTs which could not be used for fruit traffic.

HORSE BOXES, SPECIAL CATTLE VANS AND VEHICLES FOR FISH, FRUIT AND MILK TRAFFIC

Passenger-rated meat traffic was minimal and no BR stock was built to cater for it.

Milk traffic was complicated by the fact that the tanks, either fixed or towed, were owned by the companies and this will be explored in the relevant section in more detail.

Traffic in churns was a different matter. Most companies used whatever parcels van was available but the GWR developed their SIPHON class of four-wheeled and bogie vehicles. The last design, the SIPHON G, was built to Diagram O62 from 1947 to 1955, and one from the last batch is seen below.

W1048, taken at unknown location in the 1970s, is in rail blue livery and carries a board lettered TO WORK BETWEEN PADDINGTON AND PLYMOUTH. This vehicle is listed as being converted to a newspaper van in 1972 and this view probably shows it before modifications (see later text). (D Larkin collection, courtesy John Lewis)

The Special Cattle Van (or Prize Cattle Van) was used to convey prize bulls, with a herdsman, from one place to another. To cater for this traffic, BR inherited a number of different designs, some ancient and some quite modern and a small number of additional vehicles were built after 1948 to add to the fleet. These were not new designs and will be dealt with in the main text.

HB (Horse Boxes)

Before examining the types of horse box operated in BR days, the precise traffics need to be established.

The conveyance of horses, either personal mounts or carriage horses, dates back to the early days of the UK railway system and can be generally associated with the movements of the aristocracy and nobility between London and their various country estates, which eventually came to include Scotland. Such vehicles were always fitted with passenger equipment and always had accommodation for a groom and space for fodder. Individual vehicles could sometimes be seen in the 1950s and 1960s, as seen below.

A4 4-6-2 60012, taken at Newcastle Central in 1958, is seen leaving with a horse box as the leading vehicle of the train. The vehicle appears to be an ex-GWR Diagram N16 horse box and would have been in crimson livery. (Photograph courtesy HMRS, Ref ADL726)

Two other activities emerged during the Victorian era, horse racing and fox hunting, both sports heavily supported by Victoria's heir, the Prince of Wales, later King Edward VII.

Farm horses would not have featured much but circus horses would and my only recorded horse box use was for Billy Smart's Circus in 1970.

HORSE BOXES, SPECIAL CATTLE VANS AND VEHICLES FOR FISH, FRUIT AND MILK TRAFFIC

Former LMS designs

The LMS produced 573 horse boxes between 1926 and 1938 and this seems to account for the fact that no pre-Grouping vehicles from constituent companies lasted any length of time after Nationalisation. All designs were very similar and numbers were as follows:

M42000M to M42048M (Diagram D1878, withdrawn between 1954 and 1961)

M42049M to M42098M (Diagram D1956, withdrawn between 1956 and 1961)

M42099M to M42408M (Diagram D1879, withdrawn between 1957 and 1962)

M42409M to M42520M (Diagram D1956, withdrawn 1962)

M42521M to M42523M (Diagram D1952, withdrawn 1962)

M42524M to M42573M (Diagram D1972, withdrawn between 1962 and 1966)

M42425M, taken at an unknown location and date, is a D1956 horse box in crimson livery. The fact that the door droplights on both sides are lowered seems to indicate a vehicle still in use. (Photograph courtesy HMRS, Ref AA-G318)

Further vehicles were built after Nationalisation at Derby Works from 1948 until 1951 and numbers were as follows:

M42574M to M42689M (Diagram D2125, withdrawn between 1963 and 1966)

M42557, taken at an unknown location and date, is a D1972 horse box in crimson livery. This view shows that even communication cord equipment was fitted to this class of vehicle. (Photograph courtesy HMRS, Ref ABQ414)

M42675, taken at an unknown location and date, is a D2125 horse box in crimson livery. The buffer type is the only notable change. (Photograph courtesy Roger Carpenter)

HORSE BOXES, SPECIAL CATTLE VANS AND VEHICLES FOR FISH, FRUIT AND MILK TRAFFIC

LNER Origins

Unlike the LMS, which built a substantial number of horse boxes, the LNER seems less well supplied with modern designs at Nationalisation and bequeathed a plethora of non-standard designs to BR, as the following view shows.

Taken at Melton Constable, in April 1957, shown are E2261E on the extreme left, E2111 (an ex-GNSR six-wheeled design from the batch E2108 to E2113), an ex- NER Diagram 196 vehicle and an ex-LMS vehicle. (Photograph courtesy HMRS, Ref ADT428)

It has also proved difficult to establish just how many, and to what designs, the LNER actually built. If numbers carried are taken into account, vehicles of 21ft 0in length were built first and were numbered in the 2201-2279 range. These were apparently followed by 2336-2365 in 1938, built to Diagram 5 and 22ft 0in long. The design was revived, and slightly lengthened, in 1954/55 with 2391-2510, which were given an LMR diagram D2181.

This section will offer photographs and such details that are available but the full story is yet to be told.

E810, taken at Stratford in the 1950s, is an ex-GNR horse box probably dating from 1917. Livery is weathered crimson. (Photograph courtesy HMRS, Ref ADU319)

E1862, taken at Stratford in 1956, is an ex-NBR horse box dating from 1911. Livery is weathered crimson. (Photograph courtesy HMRS, Ref ADT419)

HORSE BOXES, SPECIAL CATTLE VANS AND VEHICLES FOR FISH, FRUIT AND MILK TRAFFIC

E395, taken at an unknown location and date, is an ex-NER Diagram 196 horse box dating from 1913. Livery is very clean crimson. (Photograph courtesy HMRS, Ref AAG327)

E61, taken at Stratford in 1956, is also an NER Diagram 196 horse box. It is in weathered crimson livery. (Photograph courtesy HMRS, Ref ADT819)

E592 and E8, taken at Hornsey in 1956, show both sides of the ex-NER Diagram 196 horse box. Livery is weathered crimson. (Photograph courtesy HMRS, Ref ADT903)

E2279E, taken at Taunton on 15th June 1962, is one of the mystery 21ft 0in LNE-built horse boxes numbered E2201E to E2279E; livery is crimson. (Photograph by AE West, courtesy Wessex Collection (MS King))

E2354E, taken at Templecombe on 18th August 1963, is definitely an LNE-built Diagram 5 horse box and is in crimson livery. (Photograph by AE West, courtesy Wessex Collection (MS King))

E2439E, taken at Barnstaple Junction on 13th August 1962, is a BR-built D2181 horse box in crimson livery, full details for this class on the next page. (Photograph by AE West, courtesy Wessex Collection (MS King))

HORSE BOXES, SPECIAL CATTLE VANS AND VEHICLES FOR FISH, FRUIT AND MILK TRAFFIC

W2488E, this BR official photograph shows a D2181 LNE-design horse box lettered RETURN TO DICOT WR. It is in crimson livery. (Author's Ref No W2590/DL)

The construction of the one hundred and twenty D2181 horse boxes at BR Earlestown in 1954/55 is something of an enigma. This was an LNER design slightly larger than Diagram 5 with 16ft 0in wheelbase and 24ft 0in long and, despite the antediluvian horse box fleet in use on Eastern Region, they were distributed between the Eastern, London Midland and Western Regions. None were allocated to the Southern Region, although they were used over lines without clearance issues.
Numbers were as follows:

E2366E to E2390E, E2410E to E2441E: Allocated to Eastern Region.

M2442E to M2480E: Allocated to London Midland Region.

W2391E to W2409E, W2481E to W2510E: Allocated to Western Region.

Some of these may not have carried the correct E-suffix. These relatively modern vehicles lasted quite well and E2388E was allegedly in operation in 1971, which, if true, means that it outlasted the Standard Mk 1 horse boxes.

SR Origins

The Southern Railway did not build any horse boxes, merely modernising those of the LBSCR and LSWR.

S3262, taken at Exmouth Junction on 22nd August 1950, is a former LBSCR horse box in crimson livery. (Photograph by AE West, courtesy Wessex Collection (MS King))

S2831S, taken at Reading South on 7th November 1954, is a former LSWR horse box in crimson livery. (Photograph by HW Wheeller, courtesy Roger Carpenter)

HORSE BOXES, SPECIAL CATTLE VANS AND VEHICLES FOR FISH, FRUIT AND MILK TRAFFIC

GWR Origins

From 1907 onwards, GWR horse boxes were basically the same, with minor changes to bodywork and dimensions. Diagram N13 vehicles seem to have lasted the longest in their designed traffic. Most of the later Diagram N16 vehicles became calf boxes and will be examined in the Special Cattle Van section.

W403, taken at Eastleigh on 21st May 1949, is a Diagram N13 horse box which retains the former GWR Brown livery. (Photograph by AE West, courtesy Wessex Collection (MS King))

W425W, taken at an unknown location and date, is a Diagram N13 horse box in crimson livery. (Photograph courtesy HMRS, Ref ABY117)

BR Standard Mk 1 Horse Boxes

In a surprising move, a brand new horse box, to BR Mk 1 coaching stock standards was issued with Lot number 30146, to Diagram 751, in January 1954.

For unexplained reasons, they did not arrive until October 1958 and they saw very little use. It could be seriously postulated that they were unnecessary. The Earlestown works was chosen to build them and they were already building the vehicles listed on page 14. These horse boxes were distributed amongst the three regions that most needed them. The Southern Region, although they received a large batch, could not make full use of them due to the clearance issues between Tonbridge and Hastings via Battle.

Numbers were as follows:
M96300 to M96304
E96305 to E96354
W96355 to W96358
S96359 to S96414

E96351, taken at an unknown location and date, stands in a line of similar vehicles and is possibly in storage. It is in crimson livery and is lettered RETURN TO NEWCASTLE. (Photograph courtesy RHG Simpson)

HORSE BOXES, SPECIAL CATTLE VANS AND VEHICLES FOR FISH, FRUIT AND MILK TRAFFIC

E96349, possibly taken at Crewe on an unknown date, is a Diagram 751 Mk 1 horse box in weathered crimson livery. The lettering is illegible. (D Larkin Collection)

S96413, taken at Woodhams yard, Barry in February 1972, is about to be broken up. External condition and SR green livery is quite good. (Author's Ref No W3967/DL)

DE321107, taken at York Leeman Road on 20th March 1978, was E96305 and is in light green livery with yellow doors. It is the support vehicle for the gauging unit on the left. (Author's Ref No W6855/DL)

Fish Vans

In these days of overfishing and quotas, it is easy to forget that fish was a staple diet in the UK from WWII onwards. In the period before motorways were built, this traffic was carried by rail in increasingly faster trains until the early 1970s, when the traffic passed to road.

E75270, taken at Woodhams yard, Barry, in February 1972, is one of the Insul-Fish vans which did not pass on to other duties, possibly due to the lack of roller bearings. White livery with black lettering is retained. (Author's Ref No W3973/DL)

As I do not wish this to become a dissertation on types of fish caught and where they were landed, suffice it to say that the bulk of the traffic came down the East Coast to London, that is LNER territory, and this company, and later Eastern Region, were the forerunners in design. Both the LMS and the GWR had important fleets but they were eventually downgraded to other duties.

With the steady dwindling of fish traffic towards the end of the 1960s, the modern Eastern Region fleet also passed onto other duties and this will be covered in the text

HORSE BOXES, SPECIAL CATTLE VANS AND VEHICLES FOR FISH, FRUIT AND MILK TRAFFIC

LMS Designs

The LMS had a variety of four-wheeled designs, all of which were rather similar and very reminiscent of freight vans. Details were as follows:

M39000 to M39020, M39074 to M39219: D1885, 6T, 9ft 0in wheelbase with sliding door, side and end slats, VB or VP; withdrawn from 1948 to 1963.

M39220 to M39279: D1982, 6T, 10ft 0in wheelbase with sliding door, flush sides without slats, VB; withdrawn from 1953 to 1965 (survivors to wagon fleet).

M39280 to M39379: D1886, 6T, 10ft 0in wheelbase with sliding door, two end louvre vents, VB or VP; withdrawn from 1958 to 1965 (survivors to wagon fleet).

M39380 to M39439: D1887, 6T, 10ft 0in wheelbase with sliding door, two side vents, VB, withdrawn from 1959 to 1965 (survivors to wagon fleet).

M39440 to M39514: D2059, 6T, 10ft 0in wheelbase with sliding door, no vents, VB with steam pipe, withdrawn from 1959 to 1965 (survivors to wagon fleet).

M39515 to M39549: D2107, 6T, 10ft 6in wheelbase with sliding door, no vents, VB with steam pipe, withdrawn from 1958 to 1965 (survivors to wagon fleet).

M39464, taken at Crianlarich on an unknown date, is a D2107 fish van still in crimson livery. Note the destination and consignee; Broad Street is close to Billingsgate, London's fish market. (Photograph by Don Rowland, courtesy S4 Society)

These vans were used on the slower, West Coast services and single vehicles would often be seen on passenger trains. The later vehicles were replaced on fish traffic from 1965.

After World War Two, the L. M. S. introduced a six-wheel version of their final four-wheeled design, to Diagram D2115 and capacity 6T. The L. M. S. defined it as 'Express Fish' but the B. R. code was X-FISH or just FISH. Three batches were built, as follows:

M40200 to M40249: Lot 1428, built 1946/47 at Wolverton, first withdrawal 1964, to freight fleet 1965.

M40250 to M40299: Lot 1445, built 1949 at Wolverton, first withdrawal 1966, to freight fleet 1965.

M40300 to M40339: Lot 1509 built 1949 at Wolverton, first withdrawal 1965, to freight fleet 1965.

Like all six-wheeled stock, these vans had actually been banned from passenger trains in 1959 but presumably they continued to be used on parcels trains. The transfer to the freight fleet does not seem to have meant much as even the last survivors carried FISH.

M40325, taken at Birmingham New Street in July 1957, is from the last batch, Lot 1509, and is in presumably very weathered crimson livery. The code FISH can just about be made out. Note the ancient ex-GWR SIPHON G on the right. (Photograph courtesy HMRS, Ref AEQ425)

HORSE BOXES, SPECIAL CATTLE VANS AND VEHICLES FOR FISH, FRUIT AND MILK TRAFFIC

M40284, taken at Birmingham New Street in 1957, is a Lot 1445 fish van. Livery is weathered crimson and the chalked inscription appears meaningless. (Photograph courtesy HMRS, Ref ABW227)

M40290M, taken at Millerhill Yard in the 1960s, is very unusual. It appears to be a standard Lot 1445 van but it is the white livery with black lettering for insulated stock. It also has an unusual number suffix and X-FISH code. (Photograph by Don Rowland, courtesy S4 Society)

M40338, taken at an unknown location and date, is probably in the process of being broken up. Livery is probably freight bauxite with white lettering. (D Larkin Collection)

GWR Designs

The GWR fleet, with one exception, could be considered obsolescent at the very least in 1958 but examples hung until the late 1950s in fish traffic.

The vehicles of Diagram S6 were built in 1912 and were 21ft 0in long with a 12ft 0in wheelbase. Fitted with steam pipes and vacuum brakes, they had two pairs of internally sliding doors per side and prominent cross bracing. The BR code was FISH and numbers were as follows:
W2098W to W2113W, W2630W to W2649W

The vehicles of Diagram S8 were built from 1919 to 1923 and were 28ft 6in long with an 18ft 0in wheelbase. All other details were as Diagram S6 except that the extra length allowed for three pairs of doors per side. The BR code was the same as the GWR, that is, BLOATER, and numbers were as follows:
W2114W to W2213W, W2268W to W2288W, W2601W to W2629W

In the mid-1950s, certain vans were converted to carry normal parcels traffic. They were given outward-hinged cupboard doors rather than the internal sliding variety and numbers were as follows:
W2114W to W2121W, W2165W, W2166W, W2172W, W2173W, W2175W, W2179W, W2191W, W2197W, W2200W

Use of both batches of these vans dwindled in the 1950s and many were transferred to the departmental fleet (see opposite).

In 1948, there was a surprise addition to the GWR fish van fleet in the form of the 8T Diagram S13 insulated fish van. These were six-wheeled vans with dry ice boxes. The length was 31ft 0in. The original numbers were as follows:
W3301 to W3350

At some stage in their career, some, perhaps all, were transferred to the Scottish Region, known numbers being as follows:
Sc3304W, Sc3323W.

These vans were lettered RETURN TO ABERDEEN, were coded INSUL-X-FISH and also carried the instruction TO BE LOADED TO SELECTED SCOTTISH STATIONS ONLY. MOVEMENT PROHIBITED OVER SHARP CURVES.

This implies a general UK ban but further information is lacking.

HORSE BOXES, SPECIAL CATTLE VANS AND VEHICLES FOR FISH, FRUIT AND MILK TRAFFIC

W2098W, probably taken at Swindon, on an unknown date, has been withdrawn but is still in weathered crimson livery. (Photograph courtesy David Welch, Author's Ref No W1880/DL)

DW150155, taken at Banbury in April 1970, is a former Diagram S8 BLOATER in original condition, although it appears to have leaky roof. Livery is departmental black with yellow lettering. (Author's Ref No W2121/DL)

Sc3323W, taken at an unknown location and date, has been condemned and may be in a Scottish scrapyard. Livery is white with black lettering. (Photograph courtesy Derek Munday)

LNER and BR designs

The LNER produced a number of designs for carrying fish traffic. Diagram 83 was a freight fleet design and will not be considered here.

Diagram 134 was given steam pipes and can be considered a passenger vehicle. Length was 19ft 6in with a 12ft 0in wheelbase and vacuum brakes were fitted. The history is rather complicated and the fleet splits into four groups: those retaining external sliding doors and those fitted with insulation and internal sliding doors.

E229564, taken at Niddrie in the 1960s, is a Diagram 134 fish van in original condition withdrawn as a fish van. Livery is bauxite. (Photograph by Don Rowland, courtesy S4 Society)

Diagram 134 Vans in original condition and withdrawn as fish vans:
E222848, E229197, E229265, E229345/53, E229564, E229655, E230329, E230819.

Diagram 134 Vans in original condition and downgraded to PMVs:
E222834/40/51/64/9/75 /86/97/9, E222901/5/14-6/25/33/45/66/71, E229135/42-4/51/3/80/7/91/5/9,
E229206/15 /27/9 /36/45/56/69/94, E229321/9/39/66/8/72/90, E229401/4/14/7/24/45/56/72/8/83/90/3/6,
E229504/24/40/53/5/67/81/90, E229607/8/12/7/22/5/6/34/52/3/64/8/76, E229708/10/1/26 /31/9/78/81/5/93/7,
E229801/11/3/8/33/4/71/4/84/95, E229900/5/11/27/32/50/69/85/6/91/8,
E230004/13/4/8/31/42/8/56/62/4/70/6/7/96, E230103-5/13/6/26/44/8/58/62/6/7/9/75/9/81/8 /91/4/6,
E230202/9/11/3/31/45/9/70/5/87, E230304/7/11/3/23/6/35/9/50/3/9/64/5/7/60/84 /96/9,
E230408/12/24/8/31/8/55/69/74/7/82/3/5, E230502/10/2/5/21/4/30/3/6/41/65/9 /70/3/6/8/81/93,
E230622/6/8/9/37/8/48/85/6/97, E230704/11/5/9/25/9/32/46/62/6/79, E230811/3/4/22/4/32/4/41/2/60/4/76/95,
E230902.

The vehicles converted to INSUL-FISH are shown opposite and fully listed on Page 28.

HORSE BOXES, SPECIAL CATTLE VANS AND VEHICLES FOR FISH, FRUIT AND MILK TRAFFIC

E230006, taken at an unknown location and date, is a Diagram Van converted to INSUL-FISH and is in very clean white livery with black lettering. (Photograph courtesy Lens of Sutton Collection)

E230068, taken at Marykirk in August 1970, is not obviously withdrawn but seems likely to be a store van at this location rather than an active fish van. (Author's Ref No W2839/DL)

E230199, taken at Niddrie in the 1960s, is in typically well-weathered white livery with black lettering. One or two of these carried ice blue livery. (Photograph by Don Rowland, courtesy S4 Society)

Diagram 134 Vans converted to INSUL-FISH and withdrawn as fish vans:
E222832/67/74 /80/2/91, E222900/2/9/34/44/60, E229103/7/25/31/9/52/96/8,
E229205/10/35/42/50/3/70/9 /80/1/6/90/7, E229305/42/7/9/57/84, E229400/19/23/65/88,
E229522/47/62/88/91/4/8, E229621/4/84/9, E229702/4/9/20/48/52/5/72/4/96, E229805/16/28/32/6/8/41/9/78/9/92-4/7, E229901/7/8/23/30/48/65/75/70, E230006/35/40/1/61/5/8/88/91/9, E230111/38/54/70/82/99,
E230216/44/54/8/62/89/94 E230309/16/29/46/55/85, E230406/14/25/36/7/56/7/65/72/9 /80/6/90/7-9,
E230500/28/9/34/42/58/62/73/94/7, E230605/55/9/89/96, E230705/16/33/6/43 /59/61,
E230802/7/9/29/30/7/8/44/51/5/72/3/81/92/8.

Diagram 134 Vans converted to INSUL-FISH and withdrawn as PMVs:
E222836, E229169/77, E229254/91, E229320/71, E229494, E229501, E229724/57/9.

LNER-Designed Diagram 214

These vans appeared around 1948 and were pure INSUL-FISH vans from new. The same type of door was used but the bodywork was plywood and flush except for side diagonal struts and vertical ends. The bodywork was 21ft 0in long with a 15ft 0in wheelbase. None ever received roller bearings. Numbers were as follows:
E75000 to E75599

E75295, taken at Woodhams Yard, Barry in February 1972, is awaiting breaking up and retains clean white livery with black lettering. (Author's Ref No W3974/DL)

HORSE BOXES, SPECIAL CATTLE VANS AND VEHICLES FOR FISH, FRUIT AND MILK TRAFFIC

E75404, taken at Woodhams Yard, Barry in February 1972, is also awaiting breaking up and is one of the few of these vans to receive the later ice blue livery. (Author's Ref No W3970/DL)

E75049, taken at March in September 1969, has become an INSULATED VAN specifically barred from carrying fish. The clean white livery is interesting; has it recently been repainted in an obsolete livery? (Author's Ref No W1659/DL)

E75411, taken at March in September 1969, also has interesting livery and lettering. Livery is weathered white with a freight brown panel with VAN code, followed with an afterthought INSULATED VAN. (Author's Ref No W1657/DL)

E75388, taken at March in September 1969, is the third INSULATED VAN seen at March. Livery is weathered white with black lettering. (Author's Ref No W1660/DL)

E75226, taken at Millerhill Yard in April 1975, is an INSUL VAN in white livery with white lettering on freight brown panel. Note that all these demoted vans have lost the steam pipe. (Authors Ref. W4968/DL)

DE75103, taken at York in August 1968, is an early transfer to Loco Stores traffic. As well as losing the steam pipe, it has also acquired end vents. (Author's Ref No W424/DL)

HORSE BOXES, SPECIAL CATTLE VANS AND VEHICLES FOR FISH, FRUIT AND MILK TRAFFIC

Passenger Diagram Vans

Two designs were built. The first batch was virtually identical to LNE Diagram 214 and appeared in 1954. After 1957, the whole batch received roller bearings. They were specifically allocated to work on the East Coast Main Line between Aberdeen and London Kings Cross. The vehicles were identified by having a bold blue spot painted on the left-hand side above the code and number. These vehicles were numbered as follows:
E87000 to E87499

E87095, taken at Niddrie in the 1960s, is seen here in dirty white livery with black lettering. The instruction TO WORK BETWEEN ABERDEEN & KINGS CROSS seem to have disappeared very quickly. (Photograph by Don Rowland, courtesy S4 Society)

When displaced from fish traffic duties, these vehicles could be seen for a long time, as shown by the following illustrations. Very few, however, appear to have been transferred away from the Eastern Region and none seem to have been fitted with end vents when reallocated, unlike the older Diagram 214 vans. A full list of vehicles known to have been Express Parcels SPV vans will be found on page 38.

E87387, taken at Hoo Junction in April 1970, is one of the few vans still as an INSUL VAN, although not in fish traffic. Livery is ice blue. (Author's Ref No W2765/DL)

E87114, taken at Preston in August 1968, has been downgraded and is lettered PARCELS VAN whilst retaining ice blue livery. (Author's Ref No W828/DL)

E87160, taken at Stranraer Harbour in July 1972, has received the full Express Parcels livery with SPV (Specials Parcels Van) code and right-hand number. Livery is rail blue. (Author's Ref No W4321/DL)

HORSE BOXES, SPECIAL CATTLE VANS AND VEHICLES FOR FISH, FRUIT AND MILK TRAFFIC

E87121, taken at Longhedge Junction in August 1978, is another full Express Parcels van with full livery. The mixture of stock is interesting. (Author's Ref No W7460//DL)

E87263, taken at Stanlow on 13th February 1982, is now an RBV Barrier vehicle for inflammable loads but the remains of rail blue livery indicate Express Parcels use, as does the double arrow. (Author's Ref No W10532/DL)

DE87252, taken at Sheffield in August 1968, is the only van from this batch recorded in Loco Stores use. Livery is white with a freight brown panel just obscuring the blue spot. (Author's Ref No W1039/DL)

The second standard passenger-rated fish van appeared in 1957 and continued in construction until 1960. Numbers were as follows:
E87500 to E87692 (built in 1957 by Faverdale, Lot 30344)
E87693 to E87957 (built in 1959 by Faverdale, Lot 30384)
E87958 to E88057 (built in 1960 by Faverdale, Lot 30442)

E87636, taken in Scotland in the 1960s, is from the first Faverdale batch and is obviously not on a loaded ECML train, judging by the modified Diagram 134 van on the right. It is probably in a train of mixed empty fish vans heading for Aberdeen. (Photograph by Don Rowland, courtesy S4 Society)

As can be seen in the view above, these later vehicles differed slightly on the ends by having diagonal as well as vertical stanchions, no riveted section at the top and an overhanging roof eave.

They were all allocated to the ECML trains initially. Some operated from West Wales as fish vans but were still, at this time, allocated to the Eastern Region. As well as Scotland, these vans also operated out of Grimsby.

HORSE BOXES, SPECIAL CATTLE VANS AND VEHICLES FOR FISH, FRUIT AND MILK TRAFFIC

E87713, taken at Grimsby in September 1969, is from the second Faverdale batch and is in virtually original condition, apart from the lack of a steam pipe. The weathered white livery is typical. (Author's Ref No W1678/DL)

E87919, taken at Aberdeen, Craiginches Yard in August 1970, is also from the batch above and is very dirty. ECML fish trains were still running at this time. (Author's Ref No W2821/DL)

E87978, taken at Milford Haven in April 1970, is from the final Faverdale batch, with steam pipe. The cleaning of just the number panel is noteworthy. (Author's Ref No W2592/DL)

E87985, taken at Grimsby in September 1969, has received a full ice blue re-paint with later boxed code but patches have been over-painted for details due to weathering. (Author's Ref No W1679/DL)

E87753, taken at Grimsby in September 1969, is thought to be in white livery with ice blue patches but it is very difficult to be sure. This van has a steam pipe. (Author's Ref No W1680/DL)

E87923, taken at Colchester in December 1969, has presumably delivered a load of fish as an individual vehicle rather than in a block train. The livery appears to be white with ice blue patches. (Author's Ref No W2161/DL)

HORSE BOXES, SPECIAL CATTLE VANS AND VEHICLES FOR FISH, FRUIT AND MILK TRAFFIC

E87866, taken at Swansea Danygraig in October 1976, is still coded INSUL-FISH but this is questionable, as the location is a wagon works. Livery is recorded as ice blue. (Author's Ref No W5614/DL)

E87932, taken at Milford Haven in November 1975, is coded INSULATED VAN, but, unlike the early vans, is not barred from fish traffic. Livery is dirt plus ice blue panels. (Author's Ref No W5260/DL)

M87897, taken at Derby in August 1980, represents the vans after fish traffic. It is in rail blue for Express Parcels, is allocated to the LMR but, before condemnation, had become a VXV freight van. (Author's Ref No W10249/DL)

Once redundant in fish traffic, these relatively modern vans were cleaned and recycled as SPV Express Parcels vans. This process had, in fact, started before the end of fish traffic in the early 1970s.

E87719, taken at Wisbech in September 1969, is an early rendition of the Special Parcels Van (SPV) livery. The colour is rail blue and the MAXUMUM SPEED lettering was probably applied in error. (Author's Ref No W1802/DL)

The following vehicles are known to have been Express Parcels SPV vans allocated to the ER, the LMR or the WR. Being out of gauge between Tonbridge and Battle, none were allocated to the SR.

E87000 to E87499 series: E87000-4/6/8-10/2/3/5-7/22/3/7/9/34/5/7-40/2/4-7/9-56/8-60/2-4/7-74/7-80/2-92/5/8/9, E87102/4/5/7/8/10/2-4/6/8-22/4-9/32-4/6/8-43/6-50/2/3/5-7/9/60/2-4/ 6/8/71-7/80/-2/5-8/90-2/5/6/9, E87200/1/3-5/9/11-6/8/9/21/3/6-9/31-5/8-42/4/5/7-50/3-6/8/9/ 61-3/7-74, E87330/44; M87026, M87225; W87007/11/9/21/8/32/43/8/65/6/75/81/96, W87100//6/9/17/31/5/44/5/58/67/9/79/89/93/4/7/8, W87207/10/20/4/36/7/43/6/57/64.

HORSE BOXES, SPECIAL CATTLE VANS AND VEHICLES FOR FISH, FRUIT AND MILK TRAFFIC

E87500 to E88057 series: E87500-6/8/10/1/3/7/20-32/4/5/7-40/2-9/51/2/5/7-60/2-4/8-70/3-8/80-4/6-8/91-4/6-9, E87600/1/3-5/7/8/11-8/23-8/30/2-7/9-43/6/8/50-4/6/8/60/2/3/9/73/5 /83/4/99, E87702/3/5-8 /10/3-6/8/9/21/7/9/30/2/43-6/8/9/52-5/63/7/8/71/5-8/80/4/9 /92/3/6/7/9, E87801/6/8/10/2/5/8/21/2/7/8/32-4/6/8/42/4/7/50/3/4/6/8/60/4/7/72/3/5/7/8/85-91/4, E87902/4/5/7/10/1/5/7/20/5/8-30/3/4/7/9-46/8/51/3/4/6/61/5-71/4/5/7/804/6-8/91/6-9, E88000/1/5/8/9/12-5/7-9/22/3/5/6/30/3/8/41/2/4/7/50/3-7; M87610/64; W87507/9/12/4-6/33/6/41/50/6/61/7/72/9/85/9/95, W87602/6/9/19/29/31/44/5/53/70/1/4/8/80/90/1/7/8, W87701/9/12/37/8/42/73/82/5/98, W8780217/39/55/9/61/95/7, W87931/6/55/64/72/3/95, W88004/16/29/34/46.

M87610, taken at Hemel Hempstead in March 1978, is one of the handful allocated to the London Midland Region as Express Parcels. Seen here in rail blue livery, it has the NRV code. Under the TOPS coding system, the SPV code previously used was ineligible, being for a vacuum-braked plate wagon, and NRV was the generic parcels van code used instead. (Author's Ref No W7436/DL)

By the time the photograph above was taken, these vehicles were being displaced. They had been especially popular with the GPO for their traffic as they could be made secure very easily.

Some were scrapped, others passed into barrier van usage for railtanks as can be seen from the next series of photographs.

E87847, taken at Sheffield Midland in August 1968, was an early transfer to an SPV, in full rail blue livery. Instructions have been erased except for MT for "Empty". (Author's Ref No W1040/DL)

E87908, taken at Stanlow on 13th February 1982, is an unusual survivor in very dirty white livery with the vestiges of a blue spot. It is in use as an RBV for rail-tanks. (Author's Ref No W10513/DL)

E87857, taken at Stanlow on 13th February 1982, is also still in white livery as an RBV but no blue spot can be seen. The reason for their use, an LPG railtank, is on the left. (Author's Ref No W10512/DL)

HORSE BOXES, SPECIAL CATTLE VANS AND VEHICLES FOR FISH, FRUIT AND MILK TRAFFIC

E87820, taken at Derby in July 1980, has been withdrawn. It is also in dirty white livery with blue spot and carries the interesting code "BARRIER WAGON". (Author's Ref No W10246/DL)

E87620, taken at Derby in July 1980, is another withdrawn RBV, this time in freight brown livery with RBV code. The reason for this obvious cull of this class in 1980 is unknown. (Author's Ref No W10247/DL)

E87720, taken at Derby in July 1980, is the third withdrawn RBV at Derby. Livery is freight brown and it may be significant that all these vans are Eastern Region vehicles. (Author's Ref No W10248/DL)

W87985, taken at Ripple Lane Yard in April 1980, retains rail blue livery but is now coded RBV and has specific instructions concerning use. (Author's Ref No W10251/DL)

W87773, taken at Ripple Lane Yard in April 1980, is an RBV in freight brown livery. The instruction probably refers to explosive traffic rather than rail-tanks. (Author's Ref No W10252/DL)

W87573, taken at Stanlow on 13th February 1982, is a rail blue van with interesting "CODERBV" appellation. It is barrier to an LPG tank. (Author's Ref No W10493/DL)

HORSE BOXES, SPECIAL CATTLE VANS AND VEHICLES FOR FISH, FRUIT AND MILK TRAFFIC

W87715, taken at Stanlow on 13th February 1982, as an RBV to an LPG tank, is still in rail blue livery but the code is painted on a freight brown panel. Note the method of securing the doors to prevent loading. (Author's Ref No W10494/DL)

M87664, taken at Stanlow on 13th February 1982, is rather different. An RBV in clean Freight Brown, it has no door security and is operating with a converted ULV Ale Pallet wagon. (Author's Ref No W10499/DL)

M87832, taken at Kings Lynn on 11th March 1984, is seen in freight brown livery and is technically still operational. This was the last ex-Fish van I recorded. (Author's Ref No W13731/DL)

Fruit Vans (Passenger Rated)

The Great Western Railway was the only company to operate fruit vans on passenger trains, presumably mostly from the Vale of Evesham. These vans were similar in design to the same company's fish vans and the final design, the FRUIT D, was built as 1960. In truth, certainly in the case of the FRUIT D, these vehicles served as PMVs when not in fruit traffic.

W2377, taken at an unknown location and date, is a Diagram Y2 Fruit Van from one of the last batches, with only the top planks louvred for ventilation. Possibly taken in 1951, the chalked markings ELY and MARCH suggest a fruit use in East Anglia. (Photograph courtesy Roger Carpenter)

Diagram Y2 vans were built at the turn of the century but appear to have still been in use in the early 1950s.

Diagram Y3 vans were longer, with two sliding doors. They closely resembled W2098W, the fish van seen on page 25, and were numbered W2401W to W2500W.

Diagram Y9 vans were coded FRUIT C. Dimensionally similar to Y3, they were much more modern, being built in the late 1930s. They were numbered W2803W to W2832W and W2847W to W2866W. They all appear to have been withdrawn before 1968, which is a bit surprising but could be due to the comparatively short wheelbase on passenger trains.

HORSE BOXES, SPECIAL CATTLE VANS AND VEHICLES FOR FISH, FRUIT AND MILK TRAFFIC

W2804W, taken at an unknown location and date, is a weathered, crimson liveried, example of the FRUIT C that has recently visited the SR at St Leonards and Hastings. (Photograph by Roye England, courtesy Pendon Museum)

W2807, taken at Cheddar, circa 1948-50, is a FRUIT C in heavily-weathered livery, which could be GWR brown, given the date. (Photograph by Joe Moss, courtesy Roger Carpenter)

W2857W (possibly taken at Swindon, on an unknown date, is a FRUIT C in weathered crimson livery. Although now withdrawn, chalked markings indicate last use on Reading Parcels post. (D Larkin Collection)

The Fruit D design first appeared in 1939 with Diagram Y11. These vehicles were 28ft 6in long with a four-wheeled 18ft 0in wheelbase. The side doors per side were provided, and the ratchet brake used on the Y9 vans was finally dropped, after being banned after 1923 by the RCH, in favour of a lever type. The number ranges of these are slightly doubtful, but the first batch appears to have been as follows:
W2867W to W2916W

This batch follows from the Y9 series but the next batch appears to precede the Y2 range. This number range appears to have been as follows:
W2289W to W2322W

W2298W, taken at Earlestown in August 1970, is from Diagram Y11 and is a late survivor in crimson livery. The MAX SPEED 45 MPH instruction was the direct result of the derailment of one of these vans in the mid-1960s, as mentioned on page 48 of Volume 1 of this series. (Author's Ref No W2435/DL)

HORSE BOXES, SPECIAL CATTLE VANS AND VEHICLES FOR FISH, FRUIT AND MILK TRAFFIC

W2321W, taken at Peterborough in June 1968, is in clean rail blue livery and is still in general parcels traffic without restrictions. This lack of a speed instruction probably means that the accident report on the FRUIT D derailment mention opposite had not yet been published. (Author's Ref No W425/DL)

Diagram Y14 was the next variant and the only change was the replacement of the early shell pattern roof vents with the torpedo pattern. All these were delivered after Nationalisation, the batches being as follows:
W3401W to W3478W
W92000 to W92064 (Lot 30345, built by Swindon in 1956)
W92065 to W92114 (Lot 30383, built by Swindon in 1960)

I did not record one after 1969 and I do not know what happened to this fleet. Some certainly became departmental vans but none appear to have remained in the revenue fleet, even as barrier vehicles.

W3463W, taken at Wisbech in September 1969, has retained weathered crimson with speed instruction. Although with PARCELS MAIL sticker, it was probably stored for fruit traffic. (Author's Ref No W1801/DL)

W3431W, taken at Chester in August 1968, is in very new rail blue livery and does not have any speed restrictions, thus still being in parcels traffic. The very positive coding for passenger duties is noteworthy. (Author's Ref No W690/DL)

W92012W, taken at Wisbech in September 1969, is also in rail blue livery but with speed instruction and unusual lettering. The W-suffix was not required but was usually applied. The "Observer Sunday Supplement" has been a recent load. (Author's Ref No W1803/DL)

Special Cattle Vans and Calf Boxes

British Railways inherited special cattle vans from all four companies, although not in vast numbers, and even produced some to three pre-Nationalisation designs after 1948.

Calf boxes were a curious Western Region reclassification of their Diagram N16 horse boxes.

This view, taken at an unknown location and date, is a very good comparison between horse box and special cattle van. The horse box, M42672 on the left, has the groom's compartment next to the horse compartment, to allow constant monitoring, and a fodder compartment at the opposite end. The special cattle van, M48391 on the right, has two beast compartments and a herdsman compartment at the end. Close monitoring was not required, and neither was fodder. (Photograph courtesy HMRS, Ref ABW229)

Unlike horses, cattle were for eating in one form or another. Special Cattle Vans, or to give them their earlier title, Prize Cattle Vans would generally have carried pedigree bulls from markets to farms a long way away.

Calf boxes appear only in the Western Region fleet and the only known photographs record different allocations, Dawlish, Oxford and Swindon Junction. Whether these were pedigree calves is unclear but they did have both herdsman and fodder locker.

The LNER did not apparently build any standard special cattle vans but examples of pre-Grouping designs, all rather similar in appearances and some built after 1923, are illustrated on the opposite page.

The LMS did develop a standard design and these were numbered as follows:

M43800 to M43849 (Diagram D1876, built 1926-28, withdrawn from 1955 to 1961)
M43850 to M43874 (Diagram D1877, built 1930-35, withdrawn from 1959 to 1965)
M43875 to M43899 (Diagram D1877, built in 1952 by Earlestown, first withdrawal 1963, all gone soon after)

M43899, taken at Tring on 20th November 1966, was the last SCV built to this design and, as can be seen, has been withdrawn. Livery is very weathered crimson. (Photograph courtesy JP Alsop)

HORSE BOXES, SPECIAL CATTLE VANS AND VEHICLES FOR FISH, FRUIT AND MILK TRAFFIC

E1068, taken at Loughton Junction in September 1955, is an ex-GCR special cattle van in crimson livery. The vehicle on the right is a horse box, the two types usually being stored together. (Photograph courtesy HMRS, Ref ADV032)

E1144, taken at Channelsea Sidings in 1956, is an ex-GER special cattle van built in 1913, others to this design being E1126 to E1210. Livery is crimson. (Photograph courtesy HMRS, Ref ADV421)

E2224, taken at Channelsea Sidings in 1956, is an LNER variation of an NER design built in 1927, similar vans being E2201 to E2226. Livery is crimson. (Photograph courtesy HMRS, Ref ADU002)

SR-designed stock

The LMS vehicles and two of the LNER constituent designs had the herdsman's compartment at one end. The GCR design had the herdsman's compartment between to compartments for the beasts and both the SR and GWR designs used this pattern as well.

3700, taken at Stewarts Lane on 28th May 1949, is an SR Diagram 3141 special cattle van built in 1930 and withdrawn in December 1962. It is still in Southern Railway Maunsell green livery. (Photograph by AE West, courtesy Mike King (Wessex Collection))

Two batches were built, both to Diagram 3141. The first batch, built in 1930, had oil lighting, with a distinctive "chimney" above the herdsman's compartment. The second, built in 1952 by Lancing as a direct replacement for withdrawn pre-Grouping stock, had electric light and lacked the "chimney" feature. Numbers were as follows:
S3670S to S3728S (Built 1930)
S3729S to S3738S (Built 1952)

The livery was crimson, the 1952 vehicles being delivered so, until 1956. After this, Southern Region green was applied. The 1930 vehicles were withdrawn between 1961 and 1963 and the 1952 vehicles were withdrawn between 1966 and 1971, none ever receiving rail blue livery.

HORSE BOXES, SPECIAL CATTLE VANS AND VEHICLES FOR FISH, FRUIT AND MILK TRAFFIC

S3685S, taken at an unknown location and date, is one of the 1930 batch retaining the oil lighting. Judging by the vehicle on the right, it is in post-1956 SR green livery and a fairly recent repaint by the look of it. (Photograph courtesy HMRS, Ref ABY118)

S3696S, taken at an unknown SR location with third rail on an unknown date, is also in SR green livery. Withdrawn in December 1962, it retains oil lighting, being from the 1930s batch. (Photograph Lens of Sutton Association)

S3732S, taken at Eastleigh on 10th September 1958, is from the 1952 batch and has now received SR green livery. It was a fairly late withdrawal, in December 1970. (Photograph by AE West, courtesy Mike King (Wessex Collection))

GWR-designed stock

This group of vehicles has been poorly recorded in both photographs and written text but the following details can be offered:

W614W to W619W and W622W to W625W (Diagram W13, four-wheeled vehicles built 1931)
W720W to W730W (Diagram W14, six-wheeled vehicles built 1938)
W731W to W760W (Diagram W17, six-wheeled vehicles built 1952)

E768W, taken at an unknown location in 1963, is one of a batch of GWR Diagram W17 vans built at Stratford in 1953 and is in crimson livery. The full extent of the batch is unknown but E765W survived until 1971. (Photograph courtesy HMRS, Ref AAG317)

The calf boxes of Diagram N16, which were horse boxes, have also slipped the written record net but they have been recorded photographically, as seen opposite.

HORSE BOXES, SPECIAL CATTLE VANS AND VEHICLES FOR FISH, FRUIT AND MILK TRAFFIC

W650W, taken at Swindon on an unknown date, has been condemned and is awaiting transfer to Woodhams Yard, Barry. It is in crimson livery and is lettered RETURN TO OXFORD WR. (D Larkin Collection)

W661W, taken at an unknown location and date, is in a line of livestock vehicles but does not appear to be condemned. Livery is crimson and the lettering RETURN TO DAWLISH WR. (Photograph by David Welch, Author's Ref W1886/DL)

W692W, taken at Swindon on an unknown date, has been condemned and is awaiting transfer to Woodhams Yard, Barry. It is in crimson livery and is lettered RETURN TO SWINDON JUNC WR. (D Larkin Collection)

Palethorpes Royal Cambridge Sausage Vans

Although only few in number, these colourful vans were eye-catching. The firm despatched their products from Dudley, Worcestershire, near Birmingham, and continued to do so until the mid-1960s.

LMS 38733 is an official view of the Diagram D1955 van built in 1936 but it shows the livery and markings of this fleet. (Photograph courtesy HMRS, Ref AAB706)

The company was served by two railway companies, the GWR and the LMS, and the following details record the various batches:
M38730 to M38731 (Diagram D1958, four-wheeled vans built 1936, withdrawn 1967. Possibly PMVs from 1956)
M38732 to M38735 (Diagram D1955, six-wheeled vans built 1936, withdrawn 1966)
M38873 to M38876 (Diagram D2001, bogie vans built 1938, withdrawn 1967)
M38877 to M38878 (Diagram D1957, bogie vans built 1936, withdrawn 1967)
W2801W to W2802W (Diagram O47, six-wheeled vans built 1936, probably withdrawn 1966)

HORSE BOXES, SPECIAL CATTLE VANS AND VEHICLES FOR FISH, FRUIT AND MILK TRAFFIC

M38732, taken at an unknown location and date, is a Diagram D1955 van. Livery of these vehicles in BR days is thought to have been maroon with yellow PALETHORPES. (Photograph courtesy HMRS, Ref AAX829)

W2801W, taken at an unknown location and date, is a Diagram O46 van and is presumably in the same livery as that above. The sausage symbol was in natural colours for the product. (Photograph courtesy HMRS, Ref ABG024)

M38878M, taken at York in 1958, is a Diagram D1947 van which is a bogie vehicle without corridor. The other bogie design had corridor connections. The livery certainly looks dark enough to be maroon. (Photograph courtesy HMRS, Ref ADR802)

Milk Traffic

Of all the categories of NPCSS traffic covered in this volume, milk traffic by rail is one of the most interesting and has proved very difficult to cover properly.

With the usual exception of the LNER, the rolling stock used has been covered adequately by earlier authors. I even recently acquired a 1940 document giving alternative destinations for the London milk terminals, always the main focus of this traffic, and possess a 1956 Handbook of Stations. This latter volume is part of the problem. The image below is of Semley station, between Templecombe and Salisbury. Although the facilities are obviously of considerable importance, it is not listed separately in the 1956 book because it is not a private siding.

This undated view of Semley (SR) was probably taken in the 1950s judging by the livery of the tanks. All are of the sloping tank design favoured by United Dairies Ltd. (Photograph courtesy HMRS, Ref AAX409)

At least one publication, *Southern Railway Passenger Vans* by David Gould, gives extensive details of services but it keeps a regional slant. When mentioning the Express Dairy depot at Morden South (opened in 1954 and after Nationalisation), David states that "most of the traffic…came off the Western Region.." but not give a hint as to where it originated. Finally, terminal names are clouded. One publication states that "Eltham" in South East London was a terminal. Neither Eltham Park nor Eltham Well Hall fitted the bill; the station was actually Mottingham, which used to be called 'Eltham & Mottingham'!

I will do my best with this subject but it really needs another historian to cover it properly in a complete book.

Milk Products

As far as is known, there were no modern cheese vans. There was, however, an Insulated Cream Van design which, once the traffic had ceased, saw service as a PMV. Two vehicles were built by the LMS in 1938 and they were very similar to the bogie Palethorpes vans seen on page 57. They were probably built for use by Express Dairy Ltd. from their Appleby depot, on the Settle and Carlisle line. Numbering details were as follows:
M38998 to M38999 (Diagram D2002, both in service as PMVs in 1969)

These vans had a corridor down one side, and both sides are seen here. Livery was crimson. (Photographs by Don Rowland, courtesy S4 Society)

Milk Churn Traffic

This was the earliest method of transporting milk by rail and, despite tanks being developed in the 1920s, some churn traffic survived until the mid-1960s. One noteworthy traffic was a daily van, Sundays excepted, an ex-GWR Siphon J or its SR equivalent, was from Yeovil to Gravesend, Kent, which ran until 1956; the reason for this traffic is unknown.

Most vans were of ex-GWR origin but I have also located two pre-Grouping designs, an ex-North Staffordshire van and an ex-NER Brake Van, covered in the next pages.

Most of the vans were bogie and of ex-GWR origin; details are given below:

W1001W to W1030W (Diagram O62 SIPHON G Ventilated Milk Vans, built 1951, withdrawn 1978-83)
W1031W to W1050W (Diagram O62 SIPHON G Ventilated Milk Vans, built 1955, withdrawn 1978-83)
W1186W to W1200W (Diagram O22 SIPHON G Ventilated Milk Vans, withdrawn 1959-62)
W1215W to W1222W (Diagram O31 SIPHON J Insulated Milk Vans, withdrawn 1961/62)
W1223W to W1237W, W1270W (Diagram O22 SIPHON G Ventilated Milk Vans, withdrawn 1959-62)
W1240W to W1269W, W1271W to W1309W (Diagram O11 SIPHON G Ventilated Milk Vans, withdrawn 1958-62)
W1310W to W1339W (Diagram O62 SIPHON G Ventilated Milk Vans, built 1950, withdrawn 1973-83)
W1345W to W1364W (Diagram O11 SIPHON G Ventilated Milk Vans, withdrawn 1958-62)
W1442W to W1481W (Diagram O11 SIPHON G Ventilated Milk Vans, withdrawn 1955-59)
W2024W to W2050W (Diagram O31 SIPHON J Insulated Milk Vans, withdrawn 1961/69)
W2051W to W2070W (Diagram O33 SIPHON G Ventilated Milk Vans, withdrawn 1956-65)
W2518W to W2527W (Diagram O40 SIPHON J Insulated Milk Vans, withdrawn 1961/62)
W2751W to W2800W (Diagram O33 SIPHON G Ventilated Milk Vans, withdrawn 1963-80)
W2917W to W2931W (Diagram O33 SIPHON G Ventilated Milk Vans, withdrawn 1978-82)
W2937W to W2946W (Diagram O33 SIPHON G Ventilated Milk Vans, withdrawn 1978-85)
W2975W to W2994W (Diagram O33 SIPHON G Ventilated Milk Vans, withdrawn 1978-82)

These vans are featured on the next pages.

HORSE BOXES, SPECIAL CATTLE VANS AND VEHICLES FOR FISH, FRUIT AND MILK TRAFFIC

M38680, taken at Uttoxeter in 1954 is an ex-North Staffordshire Railway six-wheeled milk van dating from 1921. Livery is crimson. (Photograph by PJ Garland, courtesy Roger Carpenter)

M38685, taken at Uttoxeter in 1954, in crimson livery, is coded BM and is lettered FOR MILK TRAFFIC ONLY. RETURN TO NORTH STAFFORDSHIRE AREA. (Photograph by PJ Garland, courtesy Roger Carpenter)

M38686, taken at London (Euston) in 1955, is in crimson livery. Uttoxeter, where the other two were seen, was United Dairies territory and these vans appear to have been kept for a special traffic. (Photograph by PJ Garland, courtesy Roger Carpenter)

E2130E, taken at Stratford in October 1957, is an ex-NER six-wheeled full brake, allocated to milk traffic and coded BM. Livery is crimson. (Photograph courtesy HMRS, Ref ADT902)

E2304E, taken at Stratford in October 1957, is in crimson livery and shows the side with the guard's ducket. It is uncertain whether these vans also acted as brakes at this time. (Photograph courtesy HMRS, Ref AEN028)

E2153E, taken at Stratford in October 1957, is in crimson livery and shows the side with the guard's ducket. These vans did operate on the other regions. (Photograph courtesy HMRS, Ref AEN027)

HORSE BOXES, SPECIAL CATTLE VANS AND VEHICLES FOR FISH, FRUIT AND MILK TRAFFIC

W1277W, probably taken at Reading General in the 1950s, is a Diagram O11 SIPHON G in reasonably clean crimson. Despite their age and obsolete bogies, these vans lasted quite well. (Photograph courtesy HMRS, Ref ABG634)

W1191W, taken at Birmingham Snow Hill in 1947, is a Diagram O22 SIPHON G in weathered GWR brown livery but it does show the type, which lasted into the 1960s very well. (Photograph courtesy HMRS, Ref AEL203)

W1192W, taken at Birmingham Snow Hill in 1947, is also a Diagram O22 SIPHON G in weathered GWR brown livery. This diagram had horizontal planking, which is evident in this view. (Photograph courtesy HMRS, Ref AEL204)

W2059W, taken at an unknown location and date, is a Diagram O33 SIPHON G which has recently been repainted in crimson livery. The van is lettered to work between in PADDINGTON & PLYMOUTH. (Photograph courtesy HMRS, Ref ABG425)

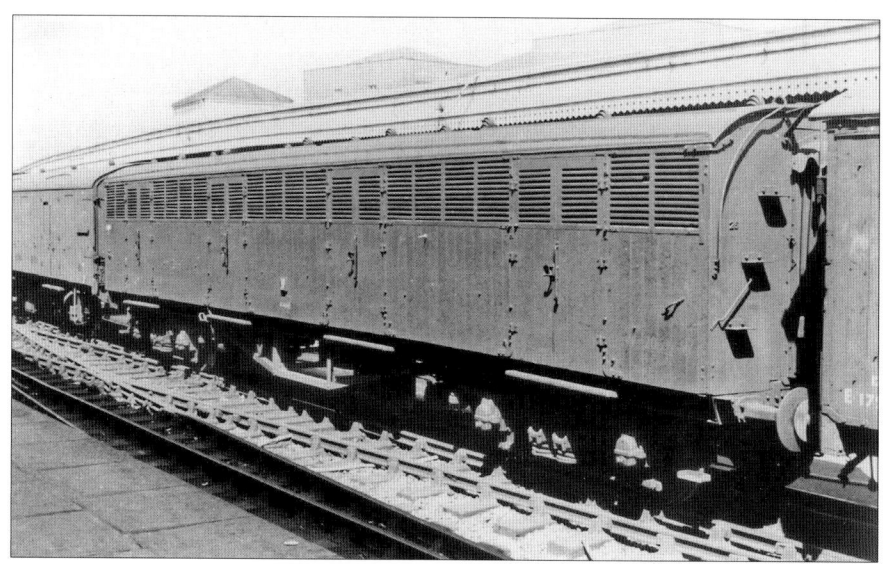

W2069W, probably taken at Reading General in the 1960s, is a Diagram O33 SIPHON G which is in weathered crimson livery. The van on the left is a Mk 1 CCT and there is an LNE freight fish van on the right. (Photograph courtesy HMRS, Ref AAG320)

W2975W, taken at Eastleigh on 10th September 1958, is a Diagram O33 SIPHON G which is in reasonably clean crimson livery. Note the lettering position, when compared with the top view. (Photograph by AE West courtesy Mike King (Wessex Collection))

HORSE BOXES, SPECIAL CATTLE VANS AND VEHICLES FOR FISH, FRUIT AND MILK TRAFFIC

W1035W, probably taken at Eastleigh on 10th September 1958, is a Diagram O62 SIPHON G which is in reasonably clean crimson livery. This was a BR built van dating from 1955. (Photograph by AE West, courtesy Mike King (Wessex Collection))

W1041W, taken at Swindon in April 1969, is another 1955-vintage Diagram O62. It is in rail blue livery and is lettered TO WORK ONLY ON DOWN & UP WEST OF ENGLAND TPO. (Author's Ref No W1295/DL)

W1006, taken at Salisbury in February 1976, is a 1951-vintage Diagram O62 SIPHON G. It is in HEAVILY WEATHERED rail blue livery. (Author's Ref No W5281/DL)

W1221W, taken at an unknown location and date, is a Diagram O31 SIPHON J that was withdrawn in September 1961. It is in crimson livery and is typical of all examples of this design. (Photograph courtesy HMRS, Ref ABG426)

Mobile Tank Carriage Trucks (for towed road milk tanks)

This group of vehicles, along with their associated road tankers hauled by tractors to a suitable station are poorly recorded. It is not even certain which firms used them in BR days but the GWR built carriage trucks for the Co-operative Wholesale Society Ltd and for Henry Edwards and Sons as late as 1947. The SR also served the CWS and also, from 1933, United Dairies Ltd. The LMS served the same two companies as the GWR and so, presumably, did the LNER It should be noted that the tanks could, if necessary, be discharged from the carriage truck without unloading it. By 1960, this traffic had ceased. Numbers of the various batches are as follows:

E70341 to E70346 (Diagram 146); E70409 to E70411 (Diagram 222); E70565 to E70566, E70638 (Diagram 295); M44140 to M44144, M44153 to M44155 (Diagram D1990); M44295 to M44299 (Diagram D1989); S4414 to S4418, S4425 to S4426 (Diagram 3154); W1961, w1967 (Diagram O49), W2501 to W2503, W2537 to W2539, W2544 to W2546, W2564 to W2566, W2577 to W2580 (Diagram O37), W2599 to W2600, W2839 to W2846 (Diagram O48), W2936, W2957, W2967 to W1968, W3029 to W3030 (Diagram O49).

These carriage trucks appear to have been used indiscriminately in BR days. East Croydon appears to have been one destination but further information is not available.

HORSE BOXES, SPECIAL CATTLE VANS AND VEHICLES FOR FISH, FRUIT AND MILK TRAFFIC

This view, taken at Salisbury in Southern Railway days, illustrates the loading method of these carriage trucks. All visible are to SR Diagram 3154. (Photograph courtesy HMRS, Ref AEQ631)

This view, taken again at Salisbury, shows SR 4426 with the four-wheeled Dyson 2000 gallon trailer tanks. These had a tow bar at each end. (Photograph courtesy HMRS, Ref AEQ630)

The vehicle, taken at Kensington Olympia on an unknown date., is unidentified but is a former LNER example in United Dairies use. (Photograph courtesy Roger Carpenter)

Milk Tanks (fixed-tank designs)

Before looking at the individual fleets, a few matters need to be considered. Firstly, the vehicles themselves were a nearly unique mixture of tank owned by the dairy and chassis owned by the railway company. When first introduced, the chassis was four-wheeled, but this soon changed and six-wheeled chassis became the standard and this was the norm in the British Railways period. All chassis had vacuum brakegear but none had steam heating through pipes, as far as is known. Post 1957, the more-modern vehicles were fitted with roller bearings but none were ever given air brakes or hydraulic buffers.

The ladders fitted and position of the tank filler depended on the company; United Dairies/Unigate was the company with most variation. Chassis livery was always black and the tank livery, which was frequently heavily stained or weathered, depended on the company. Again, Unigate was the company with the most colourful fleet in BR days. Express Dairy tanks had a fleet number on a plate fixed to the end beam. Milk Marketing Board had a fleet number on the tank side (this excludes the modern fleet dealt with on page 85). United Dairies had a plate on the tank side, the number being the chassis number; this was dropped with the revamp into St Ivel. Milk trains appear to have consisted of a mixture of various owners on the way into London and on the return journey. Locations such as Kensington Olympia were sorting places.

My own records show that I photographed nearly 70 milk tanks but none of these were at a London discharge point. Apart from loading points, others were recorded at intermediate yards, such as Exeter Riverside, Severn Tunnel Junction and Whitland, or suitable passing points, such as Swindon.

This view was taken at Totnes in 1963, and tanks from Express Dairy, IMS and London Co-op can be identified. This appears to have been a gathering point for tanks from Cornwall. (Photograph courtesy HMRS, Ref AEL710)

HORSE BOXES, SPECIAL CATTLE VANS AND VEHICLES FOR FISH, FRUIT AND MILK TRAFFIC

Express Dairy Co Ltd

In 1956, this company had private loading sidings at Appleby West (Settle and Carlisle) LMR, Frome WR, Horam (Sussex) SR, Leyburn NER, and Pipe Gate (Market Drayton) LMR, and private distribution sidings at Acton Central (London), WR, Cricklewood (London), LMR, and Morden South (St Helier) (SW London) SR.

There were also loading facilities at Seaton Junction (Devon) SR, and distribution facilities at Mottingham (SE London) SR.

Mottingham, which was opened in 1947, closed in the early 1960s. Morden South was opened in 1954 and closed by 1979.

The Express Dairy fleet was numbered as follows:
B3167 to B3185 (Diagram O64, built 1951), E70400 to E70408 (Diagram 220), E70568 to E70571 (Diagram 323), M44170 to M44201 (Diagram D1994), M44281 to M44284 (Diagram D1994), S4433 to S4434 (Diagram 3158), S4435 to S4454 (Diagram 3161), W1968 to W1977 (Diagram O54), W2561 to W2563 (Diagram O42), W2593 to W2598 (Diagram O42), W2953 to W2956 (Diagram O52)

S4440, taken at Seaton Junction on an unknown date, displays the three-star plate which is believed to indicate passenger working. The two tanks either side have this feature which did not last long. (Photograph by AE West, courtesy Mike King (Wessex Collection))

W1968, taken at Appleby West in August 1968, is Express Dairy No 93 and is a 1946 Diagram O54 tank in weathered condition. (Author's Ref No W688/DL)

W2021, taken at Severn Tunnel Junction in April 1972, was Express Dairy No 94 but has now been withdrawn for use as water carrier for the Severn Tunnel fire train. It was a Diagram O35 tank built in 1931 for West Park Dairy. (Author's Ref No W4238/DL)

W2596, taken at Lampeter in April 1970, is Express Dairy No 62 and is a 1938 Diagram O42 tank. Lampeter was not a normal loading point for Express Dairy tanks. (Author's Ref No W2636/DL)

HORSE BOXES, SPECIAL CATTLE VANS AND VEHICLES FOR FISH, FRUIT AND MILK TRAFFIC

B3167, taken at Seaton Junction in June 1970, is Express Dairy No 106 and is a Diagram O64 tank built in 1951. The faded blue livery was probably the original. (Author's Ref No W2745/DL)

B3180, taken at Appleby West in August 1968, is Express Dairy No 120 and is the same batch as the one above. Being the only batch built after 1948, it was the only Express Dairy batch to receive roller bearings. (Author's Ref No W732/DL)

S4435, taken at Appleby West in June 1970, is Express Dairy No 65 and is a 1937 Diagram 3161 tank withdrawn circa 1978. The SR designs all had the end bracing and large dampers seen here. (Author's Ref No W2712/DL)

M44195, taken at Seaton Junction in June 1970, is Express Dairy No 32 and is a 1934 Diagram D1994 tank. Apparently Express Dairy tanks were kept clean in 1950s but condition deteriorated afterwards. (Author's Ref No W2744/DL)

M44283, taken at Appleby West in August 1968, is Express Dairy No 5 and is a 1935 tank from Diagram D1994. Note that the brake levers were in a different position on opposite sides. (Author's Ref No W700/DL)

E70402, taken at Appleby West in August 1968, is Express Dairy No 52 and is a 1935 tank to Diagram 220. Ex-LNER tanks were the less numerous of the designs and this one probably served Leyburn originally. (Author's Ref No W719/DL)

HORSE BOXES, SPECIAL CATTLE VANS AND VEHICLES FOR FISH, FRUIT AND MILK TRAFFIC

United Dairies Co Ltd / United Dairies (Wholesale) Co Ltd / Unigate Creameries Ltd / St Ivel

In 1956, this company had private loading sidings at Bailey Gate (Somerset and Dorset) SR, Calvely (Cheshire) LMR, Carmarthen W R, Horam (Sussex) SR, Whitland WR, Wootton Bassett WR, and Yetminster (Yeovil), WR, and private distribution sidings at Ealing Broadway (London) WR, Mitre Bridge (Willesden) (NW London) LMR, Welford and Kilworth (Market Harborough) LMR, and Wood Lane (Shepherd's Bush) (W London) WR.

There were also loading facilities at Semley (Wiltshire) SR and distribution facilities at Finchley Road (NE London) LMR and Vauxhall (Central London) SR.

Primrose Dairy (Cornwall) Ltd was a separate entity in 1956 that had no tank fleet. The private loading siding was at St Erth WR. Similarly, Wilts United Dairies Ltd was a separate body without a tank fleet. It had private loading sidings at Bason Bridge (Wells) (Somerset and Dorset) SR, Buckingham LMR, Chard Junction (Somerset), SR and Hemyock (Devon) WR, and a private distribution siding at Nine Elms (Central London), SR. (Cow & Gate had not merged with United Dairies in 1956 and, as it owned tanks, will be dealt with a separate entry.)

Semley, and the other SR loading points, probably ceased sending traffic with the downgrading of the Waterloo to Exeter line in 1967. Vauxhall depot, which was in the arches below the station and by tanks parked in the platform, ceased accepting traffic circa 1976/77.

Tanks carried United Dairies (W) Ltd (presumably for United Dairies (Wholesale) Ltd) or Unigate Creameries Ltd, and both could be still be seen in the 1970s. Some tanks had the plates removed and had an Orange tank without lettering or a white over Orange banded tank with the St Ivel logo on the white band and Unigate Foods on the orange band.

The original United Dairies fleet was numbered as follows:

B3124 to B3147 (built 1950, Diagram O60), E70357 to E70359 (Diagram 184), E70347 to E70356 (Diagram 184), E70578 to E70583 (Diagram 333), M44000 to M44005 (Diagram D1993), M44012 to M44015 (Diagram D1993), M44020 to M44031 (Diagram D1993), M44036 to M44069 (Diagram D1994), S4404 to S4409 (Diagram 3159)S4419 to S4424 (Diagram 3155), S4429 to S4432 (Diagram 3157), S4455 to S4466 (Diagram 3157), W2001 to W2010 (Diagram O44), W2011 to W2012 (Diagram O38), W2013 to W2018 (Diagram O45), W2504 to W2509 (Diagram O38), W2512 to W2517 (Diagram O39), W2531 to W2536 (Diagram O39), W2587 to W2592 (Diagram O39), W2833 to W2838 (Diagram O51), W2947 to W2952 (Diagram O51), W2958 to W2963 (Diagram O51), W3001 to W3022 (Diagram O57), W3031 to W3054 (built 1948, Diagram O57), W3061 to W3072 (built 1950, Diagram O60). (Note that M-prefixed tanks were later given W-prefixes; the M445XX series were unallocated but many were United Dairies vehicles).

B3135, taken at London (Waterloo) on an unknown date, is a Diagram O60 tank in post-Unigate livery but without plates. The tank is sloped and roller bearings have been fitted. (Photograph courtesy John Lewis)

W2007, taken at Torrington in June 1970, is a Diagram O44 tank with Unigate Creameries Ltd plate. The roller bearings are unusual on a vehicle of this vintage. (Author's Ref No W2737/DL)

W2013, taken at Lostwithiel in June 1970, is a Diagram O45 tank, also with Unigate Creameries Ltd plate. These early designs did not have the side ladder found on many of this operator's vehicles. (Author's Ref No W2558/DL)

HORSE BOXES, SPECIAL CATTLE VANS AND VEHICLES FOR FISH, FRUIT AND MILK TRAFFIC

W2514, taken at St Erth in June 1970, is a Diagram O39 tank with Unigate Creameries Ltd plate. It shows the side platform but the tank is horizontal. (Author's Ref No W2517/DL)

W2833, taken at Whitland in July 1970, is a Diagram O51 tank with Unigate Creameries Ltd plate. There was little difference between these two diagrams. (Author's Ref No W2610/DL)

W3016, taken at Newbury in November 1975, is a Diagram O57 tank with Unigate Creameries Ltd plate. It has a sloping tank and has been "red-carded" for repairs. (Author's Ref No W5284/DL)

W3048, taken at St Erth in June 1970, is a Diagram O57 tank with United Dairies (W) Ltd plate. The sloping tank was to assist discharge. (Author's Ref No W2518/DL)

W3072, taken at Exeter Riverside in August 1976, is a Diagram O60 tank with Unigate Creameries Ltd plate. There seems to be an anomaly with the Diagram O60 tank on page 74, which is sloped. (Author's Ref No W5678/DL)

E70351, taken at Swindon in April 1969, is a Diagram 184 tank with Unigate Creameries Ltd plate. Condition is typical. (Author's Ref No W1280/DL)

HORSE BOXES, SPECIAL CATTLE VANS AND VEHICLES FOR FISH, FRUIT AND MILK TRAFFIC

W44012, taken at Swindon in April 1969, was M44012, a Diagram D1993 tank, renumbered W44012 and carrying a United Dairies (W) Ltd plate. It is not known why the "M" vehicles were given new prefixes and not the "E" and "S" tanks. (Author's Ref No W1278/DL)

W44020, taken at Exeter Riverside in August 1976, is a re-prefixed Diagram D1993 tank renumbered W44020. It is in St Ivel white/orange livery but the logo and lettering have faded. (Author's Ref No W5680/DL)

W44017, taken at Swindon in April 1969, is a renumbered Diagram D1992 tank with smaller 2000 gallon tank barrel. The former M44012 is in clean Unigate Creameries Ltd livery with silver tank. (Author's Ref No W1279/DL)

M44252, taken at Torrington in June 1970, is a Diagram D1994 which has not been renumbered although carrying a Unigate Creameries Ltd plate. It does not have either the sloped tank or platforms, unusual for a later tank. (Author's Ref No W2736/DL)

W44520, taken at St Erth in June 1970, is a Diagram D2173 in full St Ivel livery. It has the sloped tank, the platform and roller bearings. (Author's Ref No W2512/DL)

W44546, taken at Torrington in June 1970, is another Diagram D2173 tank but only has the basic Orange St Ivel livery. It has sloped tank, platform and roller bearings. (Author's Ref No W2735/DL)

HORSE BOXES, SPECIAL CATTLE VANS AND VEHICLES FOR FISH, FRUIT AND MILK TRAFFIC

S4404, taken at Torrington in June 1970, is a Diagram 3159 tank with Unigate Creameries Ltd plate. It was a rebuild from a four-wheeled tank and had early fittings. (Author's Ref No W2738/DL)

S4419, taken at St Erth in June 1970, is a Diagram 3155 tank with Unigate Creameries Ltd plate. This batch had side platforms with horizontal tank. (Author's Ref No W2515/DL)

S4465, taken at Torrington in June 1970, is a Diagram 3157 tank with Unigate Creameries Ltd plate. This batch has horizontal tanks and platforms. (Author's Ref No W2734/DL)

Co-operative Wholesale Society Co Ltd / London Co-operative Society

The CWS Ltd had a private siding serving a dairy at Melksham WR and a loading facility at Llangadock (Whitland) WR and at Wallingford WR. These served discharge points at Stewarts Lane and East Croydon, both on the SR. When these services ceased in the late 1950s the tanks passed into the United Dairies fleet. Numbers were as follows:

B3196 to B3205 (built 1950, Diagram O61), M44150 to M44152 (Diagram D1994), W1955 to W1957 (Diagram O53), W2071 to W2073 (Diagram O36), W2528 to W2530 (Diagram O38), W2540 to W2543 (Diagram O38)

The London Co-operative Society had a small fleet of twin barrel tanks. These were loaded at a private siding at Puxton & Worle (Somerset) WR and discharged at West Ealing WR. As with the fleet referred to above, these vehicles also passed into the United Dairies fleet. Numbers were as follows:

W2547 to W2558 (Diagram O41, two 1,500 gallon tanks, Dean-Churchward ratchet brake)
W2932 to W2935 (Diagram O50, as Diagram O41 but with lever brake)

B3198, taken at Lampeter in July 1970, is a Diagram O61 tank built in 1950. (Author's Ref No W2635/DL)

HORSE BOXES, SPECIAL CATTLE VANS AND VEHICLES FOR FISH, FRUIT AND MILK TRAFFIC

B3203, taken at Carmarthen in July 1970, is a Diagram O61 tank. It is not known whether all these CWS tanks had similar half-platforms. (Author's Ref No W2629/DL)

W2557, taken at Carmarthen in July 1970, is a Diagram O41 tank from the London Co-op fleet. It uses the obsolete ratchet brake. (Author's Ref No W2625/DL)

W2932, taken at Carmarthen in July 1970, is from the later London Co-op batch, to Diagram O50, and has the standard brake lever. (Author's Ref No W2622/DL)

Cow & Gate Ltd

Before the merger with United Dairies, this company had its own facilities and its own tank fleet. Prior to the merger, it also absorbed the fleet of Dried Milk Products Ltd.

Cow & Gate Ltd had a private siding at Wincanton (Somerset & Dorset) SR and a loading facility at Newcastle Emlyn (Carmarthen) WR. The Dried Milk Products Co Ltd had a private siding at Lostwithiel (Cornwall) WR. There is no indication where these tanks operated but it may not have been to London. When these services ceased in the late 1950s the tanks passed into the United Dairies fleet. Numbers were as follows:

B3159 to B3165 (built 1951, Diagram O63), M44250 to M44252 (Diagram D1994), W1978 to W1983 (Diagram O55), W2964 to W2966 (Diagram O52), W2969 to W2974 (Diagram O52), W2995 to W3000 (Diagram O52, W3023 to W3028 (for DMP, Diagram O58), W3120 to W3123 (built 1951 for DMP, Diagram O58)

Independent Milk Supplies Ltd

This company operated from loading facilities at Dorrington (Craven Arms) WR and Sanquhar (Dumfries) ScR, and discharged at Marylebone. These vehicles also passed into the Express Dairy fleet. Numbers were as follows:

W2568 to W2570 (Diagram O38), W2573 (Diagram O38), W2567, W2571 to W2572, W2574 to W2576 (Diagram O43), W3055 to W3060 (built 1949, Diagram O56), W3108 to W3119 (built 1950, Diagram O56), B3186 to B3195 (built 1953, Diagram O56) (Note: W1970 is shown opposite and is in IMS livery; one source states this as an Express Dairy batch, W1968 to W1977, which may be an error, although it carries an ED fleet number, No 81.)

Nestlé-Anglo Swiss Ltd

This company was absorbed by the Milk Marketing Board (see page 84). There was a private siding at Carlisle (Bog Goods Depot) LMR and another at Congleton (Cheshire) LMR. Other sidings, listed in 1956, were Ashbourne, Holt Junction, Martock and Tutbury, all LMR, but it is uncertain whether these served milk tanks. Discharge points were Stewarts Lane SR and Bow ER. Numbers were as follows:

B3154 to B3158 (built 1951, Diagram O63), M44075 to M44077 (Diagram D1993), M44078 to M44090, M44093 to M44095, M44097 to M44107 (Diagram D1994), W2559 to W2560 (Diagram O38)

HORSE BOXES, SPECIAL CATTLE VANS AND VEHICLES FOR FISH, FRUIT AND MILK TRAFFIC

W3120, taken at Lostwithiel in April 1970, is a 1951-vintage Cow & Gate Diagram O58 twin-compartment tank, originally built for Dried Milk Products and now Unigate Creameries Ltd. (Author's Ref No W2557/DL)

W3023, taken at Exeter Riverside in August 1976, has a similar history to the above tank but is from an earlier batch and in much dirtier condition. (Author's Ref No W5676/DL)

W1970, taken at Appleby West in May 1970, is a Diagram O54 tank from a batch attributed to Express Dairy, and carrying the fleet number plate 81. It is carrying IMS livery and does not have the Express Dairy side plate. (Author's Ref No W2710/DL)

Milk Marketing Board

This was a government run organisation which was set up in 1933 and which took over control of all milk transport in 1942. Batches of rail tanks were delivered and the numbers were as follows:

B3148 to B3153 (built 1951, Diagram O65), E70572 to E70577 (Diagram 325), M44230 to M44235 (Diagram D1994), W1958 to W1960, W1963 to W1965 (Diagram O52), W1986 to W1995 (Diagram O55)

In 1956, the organisation had private loading sidings at Egremont (near Sellafield) LMR, Felin Fach (Green Grove Siding) (near Lampeter) WR, Pont Llanio (near Lampeter) WR, and Sturminster Newton (near Templecombe) SR (S&D), and a loading facility at Four Crosses (near Welshpool) WR. It is unclear exactly which destinations were served and it may be that they served all the depots at one time or another.

Livery was originally silver-grey tanks with MMB Milk and a fleet number on the side in black but this was replaced by blue tanks with white lettering, which sometimes survived beyond the mid-1960s, when the Milk Marketing Board handed this fleet over to British Railways who passed it on the Express Dairy and United Dairies for general use.

E70577, taken at an unknown location and date, is a Diagram 325 tank still showing the MMB lettering and had probably recently served the Unigate Creameries Ltd depot at Vauxhall, near Waterloo. (Photograph courtesy John Lewis)

HORSE BOXES, SPECIAL CATTLE VANS AND VEHICLES FOR FISH, FRUIT AND MILK TRAFFIC

W44233, taken at Lampeter in April 1970, is an LMS-built tank, to Diagram D1994, now numbered W44233. It is numbered in the MMB fleet as MMB126. (Author's Ref No W2633/DL)

W1993, taken at Carmarthen in April 1970, is a Diagram O55 tank still carrying vestiges of MMB livery but with no legible fleet number. (Author's Ref No W2627/DL)

B3152, taken at Barnstaple Junction in August 1976, is a Diagram O65 tank. It is marshalled with Unigate Creameries Ltd vehicles and was probably working from Torrington. It has received roller bearings, a feature not found on the ex-GWR tank on the left. (Author's Ref No W5713/DL)

Milk Marketing Board (post-1981 fleet)

The movement of milk traffic by rail in tanks actually ceased in October 1980 with the termination of the MMB Western Agreement, which covered movements from West Wales and Cornwall to London. The following year, however, the MMB commissioned the refurbishment of those vehicles that had been with stainless steel tanks in the 1970s. If they were on six-wheeled chassis with roller bearings, they retained their original characteristics and appear to have been dealt with at BREL Doncaster and BREL Swindon. If the six-wheel chassis had oil axleboxes, the tank was removed and mounted on a four-wheeled 35T railtank chassis by WH Davis Ltd, Langwith Junction. Finally, five four-wheeled 45T railtanks were converted by the same company. Basic details of the fleet were as follows:

Six-wheeled chassis with single central filler: MMB42800-29/31-4/6-9
Six-wheeled chassis with single offset filler: MMB42830
Six-wheeled chassis with twin fillers: MMB42835
35T four-wheeled chassis with single central filler: MMB42841-55/7/8/60/1/4/5
35T four-wheeled chassis with twin fillers: MMB42840/56/9/62/3
45T four-wheeled chassis: MMB42860 -70

MMB42803 (ex-W44559) represents the most numerous tank/chassis variant of this fleet. It is in storage at Swindon on 13th March 1989 with the whole fleet. (Author's Ref No W15799/DL)

They had been intended as a strategic reserve in West Wales and Cornwall but did see some use in 1981 between Chard Junction and Stowmarket and in 1984 between Swindon and West Wales. After a period in storage at Swindon, the fleet was broken up for scrap in 1989.

HORSE BOXES, SPECIAL CATTLE VANS AND VEHICLES FOR FISH, FRUIT AND MILK TRAFFIC

MMB42830 (ex-W44544) was the only refurbished milk tank to retain the sloped configuration with offset filler hatch, although they were originally quite numerous. (Author's Ref No W15787/DL)

MMB42840 (ex-ESSO44092) was formerly a Class B fuel oil tank which has been matched with a twin compartment tank, one of five of this variant. Only one such tank was used on the original six-wheeled chassis. (Author's Ref No W15757/DL)

MMB42869 (ex-TEXnnnnn, exact number not known) was formerly a Class A petroleum tank operated by Texaco which was completely refurbished for its new role by WH Davis Ltd. (Author's Ref No W15790/DL)

Conclusion

Of all the classes of vehicle examined in this volume, only the milk fleet saw much variation. The SIPHON G vans were converted to parcels and newspaper duties and lost their corridors and ventilation in some cases. The milk tanks may have been altered from 1948 onwards, as some CWS tanks seem to have had lower ladders cut away.

The Unigate Creameries Ltd fleet seems to have received roller bearings quite early and, during the 1970s, have received stainless steel tanks. Some vehicles also had their 3000 gallon tanks swapped for 2000 gallon capacity tanks, which were noticeably smaller (see the lower image on page 77).

E1800, taken at London (Holborn Viaduct) on 22nd July 1955, is possibly a one-off vehicle classified as a Hounds Van. The nearest door leads to a kennel-masters compartment and the hounds were loaded in the central doors. (Photograph courtesy Lens of Sutton Association)

I hope this volume, and its companion, go some way to covering this complex subject. The Kestrel Railway Books team and I plan other topics in this series. The former private owner fleet in BR days is still being worked on but there are others that could be produced, such the Non-pool private owners after 1948 up until 1994 and engineering department coaches. Please contact Kestrel Railway Books with any suggestions. (Contact details are on page ii.)

The Civil Engineers' Wagons Series

This series of three volumes by David Larkin looks at the of specially-designed wagons that were used for track maintenance, operated by British Railways and its immediate successor, British Rail.

Civil Engineers' Wagons – Volume 1: British Railways 1948 - 1967
The fleet included open wagons to take fresh materials to site, ballast hopper wagons that could be discharged on site, flat wagons to convey new rails and carry old rails away for scrapping, and specialized brake vans to distribute ballast and take gangs of men to remote locations.

Most of the wagon types seen in this volume were either built for the "Big Four" railways before 1948, or were derived from them; all are fully covered. Towards the end of the period, former revenue-earning wagons were transferred into the Civil Engineers fleet, and these are also included in this volume. Finally, there is an examination of the telegraphic code names used to identify the genuine Civil Engineers wagons throughout the period, the reasons why they were necessary, and the original allocations of these wagons.

There is quite an overlap throughout the three volumes in this series, but this volume concentrates on the period from 1948 to 1967 – a very labour-intensive period, with little being achieved towards the mechanization that will be fully covered in subsequent volumes.

Civil Engineers' Wagons – Volume 2: Early British Rail: 1968-1977
This volume focuses on the many forms of early mechanized on-track plant, such as ballast cleaners, cranes and track relaying units, all of which were hauled to site. It also covers the self-propelled machines that preceded or followed the ballast trains, such as track recorders, tampers, liners and consolidators.

As for the wagons themselves, only three new types were introduced in this period, all bogie ballast hoppers, but there was a mass repainting of the existing fleet and the introduction of TOPS codes. The book includes build details, the telegraphic code names used to identify the Civil Engineers wagons throughout the period and details of the number series for each type.

There is quite an overlap throughout the three volumes in this series, but this volume concentrates on the period from 1968 to 1977 – a very different period from the previous twenty years. Local gangs disappeared and were replaced by mobile gangs that arrived by road transport. Although cranes had always been in use by the Civil Engineers, and some early tamping machines had been tried out, there was no push towards mechanization until the late 1950s, when track relaying units began to appear. These were followed in the 1960s by ballast cleaners and tamping machines. All these are fully covered in this volume.

Civil Engineers' Wagons – Volume 3: Later British Rail: 1978-1994
This volume covers a significant change to the wagon fleet. Concurrent with British Rail freight operations generally, there was positive move towards fully-fitted trains on all regions of the system. On working ballast trains, this could be accommodated by using the vacuum-braked examples of suitable designs and the early years of the review period saw the gradual elimination of unfitted stock, either through withdrawal or application of automatic braking systems. To get Civil Engineers' materials to the various depots, air-braked stock was either built, transferred from the revenue-earning fleet or, eventually, rebuilt.

Finally, the on-track plant fleet became more standardised and a new concept of "Virtual Quarries" was introduced, where ballast was stockpiled at specified yards and reloaded into hopper wagons or other types at those locations rather than actual quarries, such as Meldon Quarry.

The Wagons Series

This series of five volumes by David Larkin looks at the revenue-earning wagon fleet operated by British Railways and its immediate successor, British Rail.

Wagons of the Early British Railways Era – A Pictorial Study of the 1948 to 1954 Period

A look at the wagons ordered by BR in the earliest years of its existence and covering the outstanding wagon orders from the "Big Four" under construction in 1948, wagons acquired from the erstwhile Ministry of War Transport and early BR orders for wagons up to the eve of the "Modernisation Plan" of 1955.

Wagons of the Middle British Railways Era – A Pictorial Study of the 1955 to 1961 Period

This book covers some of the new designs that were introduced by BR during a period of great change. Block trains of automatic-braked stock were the way forward, but BR continued to build vast numbers of small 16-ton mineral wagons and general merchandise continued to be carried in small open wagons and vans.

Wagons of the Final Years of British Railways – A Pictorial Study of the 1962 to 1968 Period

The final flowering of vacuum-braked stock, and the development of air-braked stock in the final years of British Railways is covered, such as "merry-go-round" coal hoppers and Freightliner flat wagons. The effect of the change of corporate image for British Rail on wagon liveries is also examined.

Wagons of the Early British Rail Era – A Pictorial Study of the 1969 to 1982 Period

The review of the British Rail era starts in the first full year of non-steam operation, when orders were placed for the first air-braked general purpose open and van designs. A major step forward was the introduction of TOPS in 1972, which greatly simplified wagon codes, and enabled individual wagons to be tracked. The air-braked fleet was separated from other wagons, firstly by code (ABN), and then by name – Railfreight.

Wagons of the Final British Rail Era – A Pictorial Study of the 1983 to 1995 Period

The final volume covering revenue-earning freight wagons turns to the final British Rail era with 1995 being chosen as an end point, as this was when the fleet was transferred to three freight operating companies in readiness for Privatisation.

"Will be of great use to conscientious modellers of this interesting period". *Railway Modeller*